North True South Bright

North True
South Bright

Dan Beachy-Quick

Alice James Books
FARMINGTON, MAINE

10 9 8 7 6 5 4 3 2 1

Alice James Books are published by Alice James Poetry Cooperative, Inc., an affiliate of the University of Maine at Farmington.

ALICE JAMES BOOKS
238 MAIN STREET
FARMINGTON, ME 04938

www.alicejamesbooks.org

LIBRARY OF CONGRESS CATALOGING-IN-PUBLICATION DATA
Beachy-Quick, Dan, 1973–
   North true south bright / Dan Beachy-Quick.
     p.   cm.
   ISBN 1—882295–38–2
   I. Title.

PS3602.E24 N67 2003
811'.6—dc21   2002151720

Alice James Book gratefully acknowledges support from the University of Maine at Farmington and the National Endowment for the Arts. ❧

COVER ART: From Thomas Hariot, *A Briefe and True Report of the New Found Land of Virginia.* A1590–1634.B79 GE, Special Collections Department, University of Virginia Library, p. 59.

For Kristy, the needle's north

ACKNOWLEDGMENTS

My many thanks to the kind editors who first published these poems, sometimes in slightly different forms: *American Letters & Commentary, Colorado Review, Conduit, Denver Quarterly, Los Angeles Times, Parnassus: Poetry in Review,* and *VOLT.*

Gratitude also belongs to Sally and Malinda in whose lines I find such gracious company. And, as ever, thanks to my parents RAQ and RCQ.

CONTENTS

"The buildings and the Water, I wanted very much."

— THOMAS HUTCHINSON

ॐ

". . . the thought of the world whereby it is enjoyed
is better than the world."

— THOMAS TRAHERNE

I

North/South Composition

When the falcon rose the falcon
Rose to focus
The whole field into a single blade
Of grass the mole did not know not
To move
I would   my song worse   if truer
If truer my song *falconed*
My eye wide in falcon's eye
If the field narrowed as the angle grew
If the field narrowed as the tapered wing rose
I would   if truer   make my song
The cord the falcon rose upon
The mole's a student of dirt and dark
I would   my song   worse if truer
Sing in two my tongue to snap the cord
Tethering its talon to my tooth
And let the falcon free of chord and cord
Though falcon were more me than me
Was my song a feathered thing?—
How sing the sharp wing unbroken
When my mouth is broken wing?—
How be bird but sing the bird
Truer   than I   sing me
Unless, unless
From talon to tooth the taut cord could bear a
Hand not known to pluck
The taut cord could bear a hand unbidden
To pluck from song
One note which sings us both

෨෨

No grace   on tongue   when grace is   ease
I know, I've begged my tongue
To ease inside the egret's neck
To ease my tongue into the egret's neck
Is to speak at least the letter *s*
Without regret, without regret
On tongue   no grace is ease   when grace
Is breath held on the edge of a pond
I am not breathless above sheen
Am not still above the dark
Water is not wood
My desk where I am and write is wood
Where I lisp each night the egret's neck
Where I curse the lamp for sake of light
But do not dim the lamp
No grace   on tongue   when grace
Is the larch pine blind in the window
Behind my face
No grace   when grace
Eases my tongue in the egret's throat
To say   no grace · no grace
When I curse the lamp for sake of light
And do not dim
The blind tree is blind outside
In my window I look me in my eye

The eye   open   in mouth   can't see
Though blind my tongue sings vision
Though the green field sings yellow and sere
Though the mole sings falcon
Though the egret's throat uncoils into chalk
I sing myself into the egret's throat
The open mouth   can't see   can't see
The green syllable drop from the green
March through Mississippi

The earth unturned is first the earth that springs
A green leaf for a green wound sings
A green leaf sings the falcon green
Sings hunger just, sings hunger wise
Not worse   not truer
Distance is the song at hand
I sing not past my door
My desk is north at which I write
My desk is frozen water
Is breath held at the edge of a pond
In Mississippi where I did not stop
The eye   open in the mouth   can't see
The egret hunting on yellow legs looks up
When our car passed
My mouth sang out the corner of my eye
The field on the tongue when I speak the field
I would   sing worse   if truer
The field I sing sang me
Home tonight from teaching March
Rain around each branch tonight
The winter sun is red on wire frozen

ॐ

When the open eye   in closed mouth sings
No grace is grace   when tongue is ease
I keep my eye open   in mouth to see
The falcon leap from field with egret's neck
The egret's neck snakes when clenched
And curls into the letter *s*
Into distance   *slighting*
                                 sighing
                                 see
                                 silence   *ease*   *ess*
                                 shh
"S" says the snake that never was
Don't sing, don't sing

The egret's neck uncurls into my tongue
Students, do you see?—
I drove south in March
This is the chalk line on the green board I wrote
Point A is tooth and point B is talon
Listen, let's pretend to pluck the string
Pluck the string
The eye   open in the mouth   won't sing
How the song divides the falcon from the falcon's wing
As a single mote of dust expands into storm
When dusk is the wing I think I hear
The egret's cry at talon it divides
Grace is   how I   cannot see

2

Unworn

Count me among those almonds   your eyes
Count me   among those almonds your eyes
Never opened. Your mouth   on the floor-fallen pear
Never opened   your mouth on the floor-fallen pear
Count among those almonds   floor-fallen, your eyes
Your mouth   on the pear never   opened me

Open the water-glass with a shattering disregard
Open the water-glass   with shattering Disregard
My nervous   finger. I   make me pick up that shard.
My nervous   finger, I make me   pick up that shard
That makes   my finger: *shattering-water*   Pick up
The glass-shard   I open me   with a nervous disregard

What are you to me?   through the window   I see the leaf:
What you are to me   Through the window I see   the leaf-
Bare, budding elm scratch   a nerve against the sky's
Bare budding   Elm, scratch your nerve against the sky—
The sky against the window   scratched   through the elm to me
I are what you see: a nerve bare-budding   your leaf

I never opened my bare nerve   to see the leaf
Scratch a nervous window against the sky
I count me up among those   the almonds
Floor-fallen   You are the elm worn on a finger
Make your mouth disregard   that budding   glass, the pear-shard—
Through what shattering   water your eyes   opened me with me

Psalm (Galileo)

Lit by suns more million-tongued than ours
    With flames   The blind eye knows
Not eclipse   being eclipse itself   and eclipse

Blinds both by earth's shadow and by glut
    Of light   as I am blind
By sight   of stars more numerous than belief

Can bear   and don't believe, I don't—
    Nor hear that glass bell beneath whose rim
The blue stars in chorus ring their orbits

Into heavenly chords   knocked by God's thumb
    To star-song, and   now I deafen me   and God
Is thumbless, and less   fluent with his tongue

Which once sang suns into cymbals
    Comets stretched long to knock   and rhyme
Their light with larger light

And failing fled   heat to reclaim ice
    Unutterable   on Lips
No other lips can kiss   have never kissed

I know, I've tried   with my eye
    to kiss   with my eye
Distance lisped into distance   doubled twice

And twice again—   nowhere was night
    enough of night not to see
How distant, God, you are from me

Ever becoming   Not singing, you are thought
    Thinking, *I am I am*—   to my question "Where
Am I?"   You gave me glass shard for my eye

to "Let me
    See, Lord, let me
See."

Psalm (Philomela)

Breath in room echoes, Lord, I know
I echo, too—
        I breathe, I do—

I breathe to make me known to you
And do not speak
        Lord, nor do you

Speak. I think, Lord, you tongueless too—
You ravished, you cut—
        You rave in silence, too—

Cleaving the thunderhead's height in two
But thunder, Lord
        Is breath's echo, too.

Let fury be, Lord, more than pursed lips
Breath murderous
        Edges through—

Your thunder over field but bends the rows
Of wheat—my cry
        Lord, but moves motes

Of dust to my fevered chord, and then
They settle, Lord,
        On the floor

And do not move again. I cannot love
Lord, but I love you—
        Tell me you love me, too—

I cannot speak your name, Lord, but unspoken
You are mine—
            Your name broods

Inside my mouth, Lord, inside my mouth
You are a bird's wing
            I've no tongue to unbind.

Fess-Charm

Dust-swallowing dust, I am
   Covetous of
Dew, a drop. Covet the thorn
   That split in half
The water-bead into the black berry.

No one taught me how to darken me
   But me—my tooth
     Bit
The berry as the berry told me: *bite*

The wood-world, half-eaten, dark. I am
   Bone-biting-bone,
What more? A drop, a dew. For one
   Drop-of-water,
     I'd convince
The yew to bend in half its height—
   To drink, and hold
With my hand the yew-tree down.

Hold the yew-tree down. Accuse: *Do you see—*
   For one drop—
What you've become? A slave, a splinter
   In the thumb—
My ripe thumb. A splinter answers:
I am one solution to thirst.

I walked into the woods and found
   The woods walking
     In me
Demanding proof. I have a thorn inside

My thumb as fact the thumb exists.
  A thorn is
Echo of the tree. I heard, I thought
  I heard—

Myself asking—the splinter not
  Asking
Me—myself asking the splinter for release.

Said-Charm

Blood's property—the mind
    Folds leaf to thorn
        Forgets
Each crease, each crease, cannot

Unfold the thorn back to leaf—again.
    Found—not
In the half-choked leaf, not
    On the stone-broken,
        Wind-blown water's
skin—I found on me
    a wrinkled map,
How-To-Fold-To-Pierce-Through.

My warm tongue knows winter's shape—
    How to lick the thorn
        Tip and freeze
    One nib onto another nib.
A thorn on the tongue becomes the tongue's

Alphabet. Say *leaf* to tear the leaf—
    Water tears open water
        A splinter-width
And lets the ice run through. Done.

Done so. One must—
    I had to—
        Hold the thorn, pick
The thorn from the stem, first. I did

Not speak, my thumb didn't speak, the thorn
   Spoke
To my thumb, *I know the nerve*
   That knows the brain
That knows what words I'm formed with.
   Speak back, thumb,
Your drop of blood, your fluent red globe.

Hariot's Round

I was somewhere: mercury-at-zero
Degrees. Breath still rose. Last evening's fog
Around the Silkworm froze. Noon
In Mulberry leaf, noon in the Jaw:
A spring-freeze in the worm's mouth spring also thaws.
Sometime in Mussel, we found Pearl.
Our tongue in shells was nacre, too—
And nacre for necklace glows. I count by candle-flame.
I am inventory. A Pearl in the mouth is One.

&

Obedient to Raliegh's eyes: west-pointing.
We were: Jib-sail: wind-in-crescent. Moon on Sea. O!—
The *deer* do leap here as in England, they do:
A *hind* leaps from hind legs first
And bounds. Head at low branches. Brief and True in Arc
I keep my Notes secret from none. Inhabitants
Hunt with arrows. Sometime kill the *lion* and eat him.
A *bear* walks away with a quiver in pelt—and lives.
The *deer* like ours, but the snags of their horns look backwards.

To Adventurers, to Favorers, to Wellwishers—
    A first visit to this Land arrives to you on my Lips:
        Virginia. Wood uncut, miles. Full 1/3 of trees
           Are *walnut* trees; of *walnuts* there is infinite store.
There is a kind of grass upon the blades
        Of which grows silk, a glittering skin
           Already wove, until the wind blowing East, undoes it.
To speak of home unravels the tongue:
        Home. The kernel of the bitten nut is oily and sweet.

℈

I know, to entice, to convince, I must sing
    Your ear inside stone, must sing
        Gold bitten and true, the corn kernel, one seed,
           I must plant one gold seed in your mouth with my lips.
Raleigh says: the Queen knows my name. The Crown
        Of a *woodpecker* is ruby, but shy.
           Inhabitants adorn themselves with feathers, and feathers
Bright on arrow ends. Bow—before a Queen. Bend closed my book.
    The page is deaf that turns back to look at what it found.

If silence be grave, be gravity, there is no silence
Here, no weight. A god in the *elm*; a god in the *beech-*
Leaf blooms the leaf. A Native Word
For the *tortoise egg* buried in the beach
Our English tongue cannot open. Strange trees I've no name—
But in the *Virginian* tongue, Majesty, I'd speak them
Past your care. We riddled them. Clocks seem to go
Of themselves. A clock ticks. How speak but Truth to them?
Majesty? The silent minute that leadens them makes them ours.

ॐ

They have Religion, but it be far from Truth.
They sharpen stone by striking stone against itself.
They work no metal. *Witch-hazle*, they bend to bows.
Of clothes, deer-skin, and some so clothed
Think themselves *Deer*, and hide in shade, nest in *Needles*
Of Pine, and leap as *Deer* do. I made Declaration.
G-O-D. A Bible, leather-bound. They closed the page
I opened. They stroked the Book against their body;
Held the Book on breast and head. I uttered them the Miracles

Contained therein.

At Removes

—based on Mary Rowlandson's Captivity (1635?–1678?)

A SONG

Why not forge the   *thistle-in-throat*
Manic tongue into my   *thistle-in-bloom*
Home, why not   *thistle-in-seed*
Shade my home behind a stalk of *thistle-at-noon*

1   *FIRST REMOVE*

Fevered lips, they are not warmer
To kiss. They do not moan
At a higher pitch

Than the squirrel's *chit chit*—
      I hide where I hoard—*chit chit*
Fever is the fever's gift.

I tuck it in my altar.
My altar's between my breasts.
I let the rough hand go

That measures the length
Of a finger
By the length of a breath.

A SONG

Why not offer as altar the *thistle-in-throat*
Blister on thumb, the   *thistle-in-bloom*
Unsung use of   *thistle-in-seed*
The nub of bone, the   *thistle-at-noon*

2   SECOND REMOVE

beetle comfort me blight
beetle in the larch needle's sap
leaf in the jaw
worm now forest is fodder
silk and shroud
sleep unknown in coils
wing on branch that dries
moth you feast where you hide
maggot in the dead deer's mouth
bone sun-bleached bone white
needle by mending the pelt
bible in leather bound
bone my prayer my skin
sea by one man's staff broke
bible with sarah's grief
sun with stillness
wound with knife
moon with splintered light
spider now silk predicts bite
web with the blown seed caught
beetle with jaw on the leaf
doubt comfort me grief
bible with isaac with job
vein promise me lake lake promise me ice
ear I'll do what I'm told

A SONG

Why not desire   *thistle-in-throat*
The blackfly's bite, blooms the *thistle-in-bloom*
Ankle into altar   *thistle-in-seed*
Suffers, itch is need, is   *thistle-at-noon*

3   *THIRD REMOVE*

Wounded with one hand, so he healed
Me with the other.
And myself also in this

Wilderness-condition: can cull no
Beauty from the rind
But roll the walnut free from bruise

Of my foot that freed it
To bite. Not sweet, the sun.
Do you know in winter

A *winter-light*? A child can
Keep ice in his mouth as
Ice

If his mouth is cold at night
All night. My heart
Wrought on in this manner:

There is the ground, there the snow,
there is the lake and ice;
All was gone (except my life

A SONG

Limb the damp	*thistle-in-throat*
Collapse	*thistle-in-bloom*
I call me prayer the broken	*thistle-in-seed*
Root-in-puddle, the	*thistle-at-noon*

4   *LAST REMOVE*

                    let me
Math my mind: a hand
Quiets a blade   a babe
Tears at tooth   a deer
Nests on needles   I
Robin my breast   I suckle
Ice   a mouth of ice   o
How the summer in the thistle won't not bloom
And dries   a hand
Quickens a thorn   a blade
Suckles on stalk   a deer
Lies: All was: Except my—

My life). Came to the trial
My mind changed.
Do not false me memory.

I've no desire to forget.
The first tooth in a child's mouth
Is God.

A second tooth is fever.
Fever is
My daughter asleep in the barrel

Of a gun. A bullet in
Fire is
Brightness the sun?

Between my breasts I
Tuck belief.
I let the rough hand go.

Call me wife of kings—
Who told
The forest hush at the foot

Of a king?
          I'll tell you what I know—
Squirrels hide nuts in trees.

Trees are hollow. Stones keep
Tongues secret. Closer than bone.
Stones argue

Silent the road. There is no road.
There is one rock
That's throne for every king

And here I sit. Kiss me.
Kiss me. That tip
Of ice, my tongue. I suckled

My son. I suckled my girl.
Marrow is more the bone
Than bone. O flesh: O foot: you

Know
The forest lingers in the arch
I call home.

A SONG

thistle-in-throat
thistle-in-seed
thistle-in-bloom
thistle-at-noon

A CAPTIVE SONG

shal tin rotteth, I
moisten both ill
(lest this denie)
oh nettle o stain

A COMPASS

throat

noon   thistle   bloom

seed

A SONG

I   *thistle-in-throat*
am   *thistle-in-bloom*
also   *thistle-in-seed*
this   *thistle-at-noon*

Northtrue.Southbright

—after L. Niedecker

Gong-world—I strike you
                                  and you
Speak me. Not-golden—

You speak me not-bronze.

Nor am I comet
              myself enough
To hammer through to you my need

Not to be
          a speaking-ear, not
A tongue
          that listens

To each word I have not said. I can't

Solve myself outside you
                                  can I—
                                  can I

Ask you for a star inside
                          that tree
(to threaten wood) I
                would
Promise me again that tree is me.

Woodstar, woodstar—cancel
                                  out the fuel
You burn in me
              on. I am not

Made-of-you
              who am made
Of burning. I feel the tip-of-flame

And not flame's whole fury.

I'd unpeople me
For you—
Unleaf the tree I'm not—
                          (I am)
                                  unknock
The flame: unlit that wick is yet.

Now who's spark?
                  Who tinder and who
                                      flint?

Leaves more quick than stone—
                                      and then
The stones are quicker.

First forest-out, out
                                  side the door
The forest
              less wild
                          inside

The door made into the door.
I was me, most me, then.

Inforest, inforage, infest, infrost . . .
I know
              another tree grows

A knot into a wood-star—whorled
grain—
Inside the house
                          on floor-plank, slat-
forest.

Strong there—I knock
On my door's both sides
                                  at once—
Double-wilderness—

Wildness is where I cannot let me go.

Stanzas (Disclosed in Time)

One black leaf into the forest blooms
And scrapes the windows of the living-room,
Scrapes the windows in the living-room
To say, *It's me who's thinning you* . . .

I left the black leaf to the forest's decline,
Left the black leaf to the wood-rotten mind,
The fungal-mind, the dung-beetle in the mind—
The dark of the dark forest was the forest's crime

Against me. The blind leaves leave. I had to leave.
My eyes grew thin because I had to see
The leaf's vein-of-stem inside each vein in me.
Blind, the bat that caught the moth dived below the tree—

Not me. I walked into the tree to leave the woods.
I bought an oak planed down to door
And put my shoulder to door. I was allowed.
The electric lights of my house hummed loud

      And broke the forest's rhyme of leaf-in-leaf
        Budded, of branch studded to branch
      Until the tree loomed whole above my life—
        That rhyme, thick rhyme, that rhyme I was I broke

    Into my dull eyes' yearly thicker
    Lenses that made the newspaper's edge seem
    To curl when they did not curl,
                  but made words grow
    Clearer, made a focal distance
    Of the distant wars, an olive point
    Of army uniforms, made a necklace (on page 2)
    Of the bomb clasped around a woman's neck—

A distant glint (I need not
                          read the spark
That took the necklace off), my dull eyes
Yearly thicker, yearly thicker, because—

I need to see clearly to walk a straight line. I do.
I walk up inclines (stairs), I recline
In the reclining chair
                          to watch TV's gray
Chatter, let the children run, let them
Shoot imaginary guns
At me when I tell them, "No,
No, the channel will not change,"
                          and tell my wife
I need my collars starched, lest the edges fray,
Lest the dark green edge
Of my favorite shirt fray, my favorite shirt—
And patch the pants my knees have worn
Thin, and through, and not
                          with walking worn through—

With rocking, rocking, with rocking
In the reclining chair, with worrying
My hand through my thinning hair
And holding the paper steady
Whose edges seem to curl—
With creasing down the army's front-
Line into a folded page,
                          and folding
The woman's metal bomb into a silver chain,
And worry

My hand through my thinning hair, my collar
Turned up against the electric glare
Of lights that hum louder than thought,
I've quit thought,
                          I've quit thought,

I've given what thought I had to give
to children's fingers when I tell them, "No,
No, I will not change
            the channel"—
No, I'm wheezing my rhyme: No-no,
            I know—

        I know the forest's rhyme of leaf-in-leaf
            Folded, I know the mouth held open with a branch—
        I know the mouth held open with a branch
            Is the dark woods asking, *Do you believe*

One black leaf into the forest blooms?
I do. It scraped the window of my living-room
And I do not want it to.
Scrapes the windows in the living-room

To say, *It's me who's thinning you, who's thinning you*
Because you left. Because I stepped through
Woods onto the edge-of-woods and thought I knew
Me separate from the leaf that in my dark mouth grew.

I did not rhyme. The dark of the dark woods rhymed
With a darker dark, a thought below the mind—
I did not rhyme. I closed my mouth down on my mind
And walked away. Light in light hidden is a crime

Against the black leaf that into black forest blooms,
But is not my crime. Beneath the electric hum
Of 100-watt lights, then I most darkly loom,
A single leaf on a cushion reading in the living-room.

Echo & A

Speak into water,   a
Name bent at the knee.
Speak close to.
Does the surface bend
Back at breath,   am

I that loudly
Yours? Knee bent on some
Name. Your eye half-closed. That river
White at noon is blank
At eclipse. An iris, a crown—speak

Curve into dark water,   does
The surface darken
Back at breath,   am I
That loud in you, bent on knee
To speak water bright

On bright wave? A sun in edges
Ripples to shore. A day
In lines, under water, an hour
Shores in a year. Open
Your eye and the lake is open,

Knee bent at a name. Narrow
Your eye and the lake
Thins, gains speed at squint—
Behind lids,   an
Aquifer below the arroyo

Of your closed eye,   and me
Kneeling on a name.
I wouldn't speak that day.
At the lake edge, remember
The minnows

On unseen fins turn on shadows
To quicken the eye
Closed. Before: each silver
Fish its own light flamed under
Water, speak it,   a

Constellation beneath waves.
Those shadows
Were ours that snuffed that
Cosmos out
By nearing it. That darkness

Tangent to the severed wing
Of the moth—
At each wave the dead wing fluttered
And seemed to fly—
That darkness was the sun

Behind me, behind my head, speaking
A name. The moth wing
In flight inside me
Under water, to touch my
Tongue to water

I bent my knees to speak.
The sun in waves beneath us
Speaks: *wife, wish, hush, wife.*
I lake to calm. You river
To leave. Sun in eclipse,   a

Pupil, an iris, a crown
Curve, water curves the bank
Of the lake the lake's lips—
O, darkly   narrow
                             and then

O, filled with light.

Hariot's Round

The silent minute that leadens them makes them ours:
Clock-hands, arrows not-stopped. Strung on sinew, they see
Their arrow out-leap the deer; then, the deer are faster;
Or, the deer and arrow meet. *Meat.*
Leather. Custom, Bone, Bead, Belief. Raliegh stared at the Sea.
He told you, Queen. He tells me to tell you
What we see. Shoulder-high, corn grew. Then it died.
They asked me, "Why?" I could not say: *It was not me,*
My hand not burned but holding flame. *It was not me.* A lamp.

ॐ

A deaf page cannot look back. What it found
It also left. *England.* Unseen, but still, Your Majesty—
Turkey-cocks, Wolf-dogs, Ore-of-Iron, Alum, Lime-for-Brick.
Believe me if you don't believe my ink. Also:
These Native Men have *Souls.* A richer mine for God
Than us, though they think we gods. Half-gods.
We carry no weapons, Queen. By kindness we calm them,
Claim them, we convince. We leave towns and towns die.
We return in air, invisible. We wound them from inside.

The kernel of the bitten nut is oily and sweet—
And as my tongue is true, what's sweet to me is
As like to you. You: I keep you in my mouth
But my mouth is yours. The sweet nut bitten
Is never bit. Is bit and never-bit. Both are true. I sing you *Home*
But am not home. I write from this Sea Coast
Where is our abode. I look inland, where we do not go.
If no more were known than now I know, my song
Sufficient, were done. I am doubtless to make you so.

Of fears, I speak you none.

ॐ

The *deer* like ours, but their horns look backwards
At whom they flee. Look backwards and the bullet hits.
Look backward: the bow-spring is silent when the arrow's notched,
And after, is silent too. The arrow is silent in the air,
But the air is not. Air whistles when leapt through. I am not silent
Though I seem silent to you. I sing my book—not to myself.
Not yet to you. I don't look back at who my song is written to,
Else none will follow. Queen, Raleigh looks at the Sea. I am
A man in need. Arrows leap North, and then North closes. South
wounds.

East is no single point. On a map. East is where I'm needed and am not.

I sing my inventory. A *pearl* in the mouth is One.
Two are *deer's horns.* Three: feathers on an arrow-shaft.
Four legs the hind grazes. One bullet. The *deer* at Zero
Are men's mouths full. An inhabitant, grievously sick,
Asked us pray, that he might die or live in Eternal Bliss.
Corn-in-Drought, but we shared of their fruit.
A Native buried pushed his hand through dirt and rose.
He spoke Hellish warnings. He declared where his soul had been.
They think all gods are human in form. I am West. The world is

A quantity. Trees are infinite. Almonds are sweet. Most is unknown.

Work-Charm

A sweetness grows in mouth—
   My mouth—of me
     Telling me
What tree I am I must cut down.

Elm-beetle *brittles* the branch
   Not mine, my mouth
To gypsy-moth's mouth's unknown—
     My voice
   I learned to throw
Inside a leaf to tell moths, *No*—
   Starve—you'll starve
Before I let my house grow cold.

I own the arm that owns the axe—
   I tend
My iron edge's volcanic urge *to cleave to*
   wood
Cleaves the wood in two. Molten edge—
   Cooled-to-form—
     Never less cruel
Than at the first axe-swing's wooden end, how
   I learned
     To tame me
With you. Learned

A volcano's red gaze urges one stone
     To melt
   Into a stone
That thrown in water floats (pumice, punish)—
     Melts
   One stone
Into dark-glass, axe-edged, obsidian

That cuts the thumb
      That thumbs
The edge and asks: *How sharp?*, asks: *Why?*

I see on pond how I can float and push
      The pond-edge up—
How my iron-edge sinks, but ripples. I know

How sharp to be to split water-in-half. I see
      Behind glass—
         My window's glass—
Wife stir flame with wooden spoon
      Inside my house
         I own—
      Am half-owner
Of pond, these woods—am half-owned.

Vellum-Charm

Watermark me, my margin-need
   held up to light
     I would be
Owned to know who owned me:

I am not speaking, "You." I'm standing
   on ocean-
     strand, written-in-
Half. I've one hand kept
   sandfull
     to dry ink—
One hand to warn ocean, inkfull, back.

I've called the seagull's white wing
   the margin
     blank and I
Was wrong. Not glue, a sinew binds—
   torn from spine
     a wing darkens—
It does not fly. I see I misspoke.
   the blank page
     darkly

Hungers, not for ink. At ocean-depth
   a wave un-
     noticed begins to
Turn: a first page. Frontispiece: *blank.*
   Contents: *shallowing.*
     Editor: *anon., un-*
Known. In half-read books that wave is
   cresting—
     in epilogue
The broken wave is closed. A last page

Stranded turns. Seems to say, "You
    spoke me." I
        did not speak. I
Stood, half-silent, half-seeing, to read
    indefinite volumes
        cast ashore,
Spine-broken. Write to me, you I'm not
    speaking to—
    you
Turned the ocean's last page. "Speak,"
    again—"speak,"
        again—"speak,"
Breaks the ocean ceaselessly abridged.

I kept a strand of me un-marked
    for you—a margin
        to edit. I
Found me marked *lc* [lower case, uncapitalize] and later
    (you) the same
        passage: *stet, stet.*
You change your mind. I did not think
    my own blank thumb
        my distant shore—
                shore—an *indexed* bay,
Safe-harbor for—what pen-schooner, pen-frigate, what barge.

Psalm (Traherne)

I lived inside myself until I loved
    And then I lived, Lord   then I lived
With thirst   and happiness was thirst

And thirst lived in the center, Lord
    Of every water-drop   as in a seed
A mouth hungers

And then a mouth is filled with grain,
    And then the mouth becomes the field
Of grain   until the field closes   Lord, begging

"Devour me again—   with less
    Distraction."   Forgive me the sun
Eclipsed by gold   Forgive me

The gold divorced of coin   forgive
    Me the coin melted to ring   and most, Lord
Forgive my hand that wears the ring:

That hand I use at noon to shield my eye
    From sun.   An infant-eye believes
The star at finger tip is diamond

And doesn't burn   and night, Lord
    Night when most I loved
The sky's   burden was light   and joyful

The universe you made   you made
    For me alone   The new moon's tender knife
Has cut the dawn to day   At noon, Lord

I see the world is most like you, shadowless
    And impossible of shadow. To throw
A stone at star   draws me near you, Lord

Who am not separate, no   Who am not less
    Than grain devoured, Lord   A tooth can break
A husk   by husk can be broken   both are prayer, Lord

Both are prayer   As I, open-eyed am open
    To You   As close-mouthed, I speak you
Best my hymn   Lord, speak you   best my prayer.

3

Daybook

A brick migrating East
Equal speaks
Hard as one brick walking West.
A Northern brick thaws
Quick as Southern brick will freeze.

One brick founds. A multitude
(brick upon brick
            brick)
A multitude—confounds.

I.

In Babel
The minister of Close Observation
Named me
Inspector of Each and Every Brick.

My parents named me, Scrutiny.
My job: Tower Project,
Department of Attention Undivided.

2.

Mouth, our City. One voice holds
A hand inside every voice.
I noted, *Construction Concerns.*
Material lack? Open the loose-lipped mine.
Costs? Tax breathing, bread rising.
Labor? File soft thumb callused.

Yes-voice, spoken once—a mound
Of pebbles you melt to brick.
Yes-voice, conglomerate—
Brick upon brick
                brick
Babel accords. Babel nods. Babel wants
A Tower for its Throat.

A brick recommends square virtue.
Corners. Stack. Opposite,
The unseen edge mimics the edge seen.
I dream my columnar dream:
To turn corners, quoin—
To uprighten, muster, I must *mortar*.

MINE—Brick-pillows? Brick-bed? A closet built of brick,
not brick—the clothes within? Bricks as shoes I cannot wear.
Laces—with pitch—I cannot tie. More personal yet? Teeth
as a pre-formed wall. Cinder-block of the tongue bitten down.
These words I will not speak to City. This page I call, Withholding.

A city resides in the columnar dream
Of Architect's firm thought:
A Tower *thins* the further it rises—
Expect no egress to walk inside the sky—
Heaven-high, plan a thumb-hole.
Pick us a *privileged arm* to poke
The blue fabric through.

Acres apart or standing close
Two bricks agree, Sturdiness.
   —Scrutiny, we agree you do your job well.
One brick atop another brick
Their looseness a delicate lesson.

Sturdy-seeming, a gust threatens—Topple.
A blind gull worries us with Tumble.
A low voice rumbling impersonates
Steady Calm, but close attention reveals
The vibrating air should tell us—Fret.
   —Scrutiny, you give loose mouths their fodder.

Base-questions the Minister of Long Paces
Sends. I suggest a foundation
10x10 wheatfields wide. Binding-questions
The Minister of Structural Integrity
Asks. First attempt
      , ~~a distillation of snail meandering and spit~~
      FAIL
      , ~~horsehooves ground, fog-moistened~~
      FAIL
      , ~~slow water tied to wood-shavings~~
      FAIL
      , tendon of bird-wing, paper-pulp,
      mustard seed, goat milk
      APPROVED

A Tower mended by broken flight?
Permission granted.
Unwritten Tower? Red ink
The Minister of Stamped Approval
Changed to Blue. Yes-voices,
Throats clear, knuckles bent: Construct.

3.

A first brick name, Potential.
A single brick? Token, Totem.
A person alone name, Two Hands.
10,000 people? City.
A *Structure Rising*, the bricks
We call when count is lost.
A last brick name, Unknown.

MINE—A door, I don't—forget how a hand opens into a door.
Brick-face, dimpled—a flaw in the firing process. 3 knuckles
construct a finger. 2 lids construct the closed eye. Cuticle
binds the nail to the finger's prying cylinder. My palm the
Astrologer read—aloud in the city square: "A river from the
Base of Thumb in confluence with the Hinge where the hand
into a fist collapses." This page: Bending Influences.

A shoulder thickens carrying bricks.
Confirms the Tower: a body concedes.
Trowel-hands. Ease of walking
Ever upward, ankle-tilt, gradual
Slope. Close Observation? Try
To distinguish a thumb from dirt
Being thumbed through—against
A brick, thumb loses its fine print.

Construct a Tower, silence builds
Mortar-words—*right angle,*
Intersection of Winds, Trajectory of Winds,
A brick place straight on brick.

Babel knows whereof Babel speaks.

Architect thinks a fabric sky
We *bolt* to Tower-top.
       —Scrutiny, what do you say?
A fabric you *pin*.
       —Scrutiny, advise.
The roof of a mouth directs words outward.
Plan on: symmetry of sky and mouth.
Plan on: a solid sky. Prepare
A *flexible adhesive*. Prepare ears.

MINE—Before, chorus of voices agreeing, Tower, beginning
this morning, rise. Generations building. Anxiety of vertigo.
An ankle forgets how the long grass wound around it, asking
the foot to tread-no-more. Clouds as distance, cooling wind—lost.
Now, I bend my neck to descry the jagged line where the Tower
struggles still higher against the sky—careful angle, where
the sun burns a hole threatens my eye. Remember—I must—
my eyes to brick belong. Who's talking? To this page I send
my caution, Ground for Air Exchanged.

Directives to break a building silence.
2 generations, Tower
Project. We forget how to build
New hands. The Minister of Continuous
Appraisal reminds, *Procreate.*
        —Scrutiny, you agree?
A hand cannot fit into a hip
Easy as a brick lays down a brick.
I recommend, *Constant reminder.*

Against sky huddled, hunched
Shoulders, now choose
A thumb to poke sky through:
        —a child named, Early
        —a girl named, Exact Quantity
        —a student named, Aptitude
Month hence, the Tower ends.

4.

Clamor rests—brick on brick.
Hands set down their hands.
Prints on fingers again
Grow as moss on Tree grows—
A Tree stunts,
Sap-stopped. Festivity.
Circulation of people inside a brick.
Vein.

Tower-lived generations, Babel
Descends, gathers Earthward.
Throat of feet says, Trudge.
Earth left silent silence returns.
To our celebration the clouds send gray
Reservations, banquet table, Babel:
Fruit in towers now the Tower's done.

MINE—*The jagged line complete and smooth, at day I see*
the Tower split the clouds. Night, moon full, dark
brick darkens into night, but the mortar glows—a thin graph
on the sky's whirling. Constellations whirl. The Bear loses
a fore-leg and an hind each night. The Scorpion, in Autumn,
loses its bite—Tower stands unstung. Inside my eye the Tower
walks, wind blows clouds quick through the day. Slant,
I think—my Wobbly Concerns.

A Tower-language: one syllable stretched taut.
　　—Scrutiny, hear you, one word
　　from dirt to sky?
Measure in a broad tongue
Our *Celebratory Month.*
　　—Scrutiny, record here
　　Babel's joy.

My list, Festival Notes.

1. Sweet-meat. Ice melts, pools. Water.
2. Thumbless men holding cups.
   Thumbs at night stiffened, stopped.
   Dropped food. Ants dizzy, bees swarm.
3. Won't rise, bread relents. Wafers.
4. Clouds whiter as the sky darkens.
   Splitting clouds, spitting.
   Sky, half-rain. Dirt, half-wheat.
5. Lightning, faces. Flash, flesh. We don't.
6. A woman all her teeth loses and can't.
   Banquet, bruised. Green fruit. Red.
7. Ox born without knees and can't.
   Limp plow. Furrow. Brow.
8. Hour no candle would light.
9. After sleep one eye stays shut.
   Reminder of night at noon. Half-face.
   Portable half-darkness.
10. Rotten breath. Tic. Eyes red, watery.
11. Blushing. Blinking lashes. Eyes.
12. Dreams of men pulling plows.
    Flood. Fish among field.
    Dreams of wheat stiffer than wind.
    Blades of wheat. Cut hands. Drought.
13. Biting tongues. Tooth-loss.
    Moss on tongue. Swelling of tongue. Dis-use.
14. Dreams of Tower as grass-blade.
    Threshing-fear.
    Dull blades, men. Forage. Deer.

—Tomorrow, Scrutiny. Babel begins
Tower Climb.
Are you ready? Put away your list. Ignore it.

15. Brittle hands. Books. Tremble. Bricks.
16. Nervous paper. Thin lips.
17. Dream of brick as bottled wind.
    Tongue, mouth-rock. Breath.
18. Ears. Wind, an unfinished word.
19. Lost syllables . . .

—Scrutiny, High Council asks you:
Put away you
Your List.

. . . Elision.

5.

Unwinds
        Each person his own, her own

Scroll
      ed tongue, frantic. Brick un-done
                   -fastened)
                   -buttoned).

Wind, the Tree's shudder
            shoulder)—

Brightest leaf, turn a hand away, tremble.
After you another leaf waits.
Waits only on your falling, falling season.

In the mouth our story, Babel
           our tale)   unfurled—
           our page) fainted—
                    foul-fallen.

—Scrutiny, define . . .

Hawk, raptor, bird-of-prey, sharp-beak, talon
Hawk, to sell wares, rubble-profit

Sees, to grab with the eyes, to comprehend, to allow
Seize, to grab with the hands, aggression, desperate chance

Rein, leather strap to guide a horse, attached to bit, bridle
Reign, dominating power, influence, throne
Rain, crop-fodder, moist chain, cloud-shackle, thick vapor

Gait, any manner in which a horse moves, a man walks
Gate, a moveable barrier, an opening enclosure

—Scrutiny, define, define . . .

A Noise, sound, esp. of a large, confused kind
Annoys, a botherance, a wing buzzing in the ear *annoys*

Hours, divisions between the sun blinking open and closed
Ours, that which to the group belongs

Ours, each tree's name
       shrub)
       blade)   at once speaking
       seed)   co-incidence

Ours, sky empty built over with clouds
  , horse-hooves West walking
  , geese North flying
  , sparrows South flying
  , ancestors East, barefoot, the Land of Nod
                    Agree)
                    Consent)

—Scrutiny, fill with black lines
Our empty pages. Continue.

      Sky, a dark life withheld
Night, lanternless, starless—
Babel, hold open each eyes'
Lid

Another Eye stays open
An hour dilates and we
Want an hour more
        the night to hold darkness
Not to see
Babel with us and ants swarm.

A sliver with our Needled-Tower cut
Bleeds thin silver   thinner
       than the moon—
But Dark Thread sutures
Shut the wounded sky, our wound

We loved and could not utter
An hour more
        Babel asks

To mend the cheek we've bitten through.
Wound utters wound,
     Moon stutters into moon,
Everyone's mouth in eclipse
             lisp)
A blunt tooth we have
     each to bite our tongue
Ourselves, darkly
          our tongues
Tell each to each: You, and You. You.

NOTES

Charms—A sense of the magical potency latent in prayer and natural objects carried forward from the middle ages into the Renaissance and beyond. Illness, seen as the occupation in the body by a foreign presence, could be "charmed" out of the sick person by a slightly altered prayer that directly addressed the illness: "Thou tetter-worm begone from hence . . ." Other charms included the use of objects or animals: to heal a child of a dog bite, force the dog to eat a scroll on which a charm was written. A sick child might be healed by cutting up the child's girdle and burying it, tying nettles in blue cloth and burying it, or any number of devices by which language fused to object elicited a magical healing.

Sir Thomas Hariot—Hariot's *A Briefe and True Report of the New Found Land of Virginia,* published in 1588, was meant to reinvigorate the flagging interest in settlement in the New World. Far more than simply a historian of Sir Walter Raleigh's first attempt at a permanent settlement, Hariot was a man whose intellectual pursuits ranged brilliantly from poetry to astronomy, mathematics to linguistics—fields to which he contributed lasting genius. His circle of friends included Kepler, Chapman, and Marlowe. Hariot was but 25 when he came to Virginia, and stayed but 2 months, returning with Sir Francis Drake, after a hurricane that destroyed most of Drake's 23 ships was taken to be a sign from God to return.

Mary Rowlandson—On February 10, 1675, Lancaster, Massachusetts was attacked by the Narragansett Indians. Mary Rowlandson's house was put to flame and the inhabitants attacked. In the fray, her brother-in-law, her sister, and her nephew were killed. The same bullet that pierced through the hand and bowels of the child in her arms also wounded Mary. The warriors gathered Mary and her surviving children together and led them into the woods. The wounded baby died in Mary's arms; her ten year old daughter was sold for a gun. Mary survived and returned to her minister husband. She wrote her *Narrative* to document the providence in her suffering. Each chapter was titled as a "Remove."

Thomas Traherne—A 17th century Christian Mystic and poet, Thomas Traherne's major works, the *Dobell Poems* and the *Centuries of Meditation,* remained unknown to the world until William T. Brooke purchased in 1896, for a few pence, two manuscripts he found in London. His vision is best described in his own words: "Upon this I began to believe that all other creatures were such that God was Himself in their creation, that is *almighty power wholly exerted;* and that every creature is indeed as it seemed in my infancy: not as it is commonly apprehended, everything being sublimely rich and great and glorious, every spire of grass is the work of His hand; and I in a world where everything is mine, and far better than . . . diamonds and pearls."

RECENT TITLES FROM ALICE JAMES BOOKS

My Mojave, Donald Revell
Granted, Mary Szybist
Sails the Wind Left Behind, Alessandra Lynch
Sea Gate, Jocelyn Emerson
An Ordinary Day, Xue Di
The Captain Lands in Paradise, Sarah Manguso
Ladder Music, Ellen Doré Watson
Self and Simulacra, Liz Waldner
Live Feed, Tom Thompson
The Chime, Cort Day
Utopic, Claudia Keelan
Pity the Bathtub Its Forced Embrace of the Human Form, Matthea Harvey
Isthmus, Alice Jones
The Arrival of the Future, B.H. Fairchild
The Kingdom of the Subjunctive, Suzanne Wise
Camera Lyrica, Amy Newman
How I Got Lost So Close to Home, Amy Dryansky
Zero Gravity, Eric Gamalinda
Fire & Flower, Laura Kasischke
The Groundnote, Janet Kaplan
An Ark of Sorts, Celia Gilbert
The Way Out, Lisa Sewell
The Art of the Lathe, B.H. Fairchild
Generation, Sharon Kraus
Journey Fruit, Kinereth Gensler
We Live in Bodies, Ellen Doré Watson
Middle Kingdom, Adrienne Su
Heavy Grace, Robert Cording
Proofreading the Histories, Nora Mitchell
We Have Gone to the Beach, Cynthia Huntington
The Wanderer King, Theodore Deppe
Girl Hurt, E.J. Miller Laino
The Moon Reflected Fire, Doug Anderson

ALICE JAMES BOOKS has been publishing exclusively poetry since 1973. One of the few presses in the country that is run collectively, the cooperative selects manuscripts for publication through both regional and national annual competitions. New regional authors become active members of the cooperative, participating in the editorial decisions of the press. The press, which historically placed an emphasis on publishing women poets, was named for Alice James, sister of William and Henry, whose fine journal and gift for writing went unrecognized within her lifetime.

TYPESET AND DESIGNED BY MIKE BURTON

PRINTED BY THOMSON-SHORE